Our Favorite Pets

Crazy About

Kittens

Harold Morris

TABLE OF CONTENTS

Kittens 2

Glossary 22

Index 23

A Crabtree Seedlings Book

CRABTREE
Publishing Company
www.crabtreebooks.com

Kittens

Baby cats are really cute!

kitten (KIT-uhn)

Baby cats are called kittens.

Kittens love to play
and climb.

7

claw (KLAW)

Kittens have sharp **claws**. Their claws help them climb.

Kittens have sharp baby teeth.

KITTEN TIPS

Kittens will chew on anything. Keep them away from things that could hurt them.

Kittens drink milk from their mother. When they are older, they eat **solid** food.

Cats and kittens make great house **pets**. They do not need to go outside.

KITTEN TIPS
Indoor cats and kittens need a **litter box**.

15

Kittens have soft fur. They lick themselves to stay clean.

Cats and kittens have **whiskers** to help them feel their way around.

KITTEN TIPS

Never trim or cut your pet's whiskers!

whiskers (WISS-kurz)

Cats and kittens are good **companions**.

Glossary

claws (KLAWZ): Claws are hard, curved nails on the feet of an animal.

companions (kuhm-PAN-yuhnz): Companions are people or animals you spend time with or enjoy being with.

litter box (LIT-ur BOKS): A litter box is a box or tray where small house pets can pee and poop.

pets (PETS): Pets are animals that people keep and take care of for pleasure.

solid (SOL-id): A solid is hard and firm, not runny like a liquid.

whiskers (WISS-kurz): Whiskers are long, stiff hairs near the mouth of some animals, such as cats.

Index

claws   9
food   13
litter box   15
pets   14
teeth   10

School-to-Home Support for Caregivers and Teachers

This book helps children grow by letting them practice reading. Here are a few guiding questions to help the reader build his or her comprehension skills. Possible answers appear here in red.

Before Reading

- **What do I think this book is about?** I think this book is about finding the best kitten to have as a pet. I think this book is about having fun with kittens.

- **What do I want to learn about this topic?** I want to learn more about how to take care of a pet kitten. I want to learn the best toys to have for a pet kitten.

During Reading

- **I wonder why...** I wonder why kittens do not need to go outside. I wonder why kittens like to lick their fur.

- **What have I learned so far?** I have learned that kittens have whiskers to help them feel their way around. I have learned that kittens make very good pets.

After Reading

- **What details did I learn about this topic?** I have learned that kittens drink milk from their mother. I have learned that when kittens get older they eat solid food.

- **Read the book again and look for the glossary words.** I see the word *claws* on page 9, and the word *whiskers* on page 18. The other glossary words are found on pages 22 and 23.

Library and Archives Canada Cataloguing in Publication

CIP available at Library and Archives Canada

Library of Congress Cataloging-in-Publication Data

CIP available at Library of Congress

Crabtree Publishing Company
www.crabtreebooks.com   1–800–387–7650

Print book version produced jointly with Blue Door Education in 2022

Written by: Harold Morris

Print coordinator: Katherine Berti

Printed in the U.S.A./CG20210915/012022

PHOTO CREDITS:
Cover photo © Lepas; background illustration on cover and throughout book © Andrew_Rybalko; Page 2 ©Seregraff; Page 3 © Olha_stock; Page 4 © RalchevDesign; Page 5 © Federherz; Page 6 © Astakhova; Page 7 © Flower Studio; Page 8 © inese online; Page 9 © pproman; Page 10 © Dixi_; Page 11 © Konstantin Aksenov; Page 12 ©OlyaSolodenko; Page 13 © GreyCarnation; Page 14 © chendongshan; Page 15 © Africa Studio; Page 16 © Ilse Oberholzer; Page 17 © AkilinaWinner; Pages 18-19 © Maestrovideo; Page 20 © Astakhova; Page 21 © adogslifephoto.Page 22 © vizland, © adogslifephoto, © Africa Studio, © AkilinaWinner; Page 23 © OlyaSolodenko, © Arthur Francescato   All photos from Shutterstock.com and Istockphoto.com

Published in the United States
Crabtree Publishing
347 Fifth Ave.
Suite 1402-145
New York, NY 10016

Published in Canada
Crabtree Publishing
616 Welland Ave.
St. Catharines, Ontario
L2M 5V6